EDGBA

AS IT

By Douglas V. Jones

*A place steeped in history and an
enviable enclave of sylvan beauty*

The River Rea at Edgbaston, 1898

PUBLISHED BY

Westwood Press Publications

PRINT SHOP, 44 BOLDMERE ROAD, SUTTON COLDFIELD
WEST MIDLANDS   TELEPHONE 021-354 5913

1

Birmingham University Campus in 1986

Acknowledgments

The author and publisher wish to thank Mr. Patrick Baird of Birmingham Central Library, Local Studies Department for his help in lending many of the illustrations in this book. They also gratefully acknowledge the assistance given by Mr. John Meering of the Calthorpe Estate Office; Mr. W.R. Clarke of Harborne Library; Mr W.A. Camwell; Mr Ken Kelly; Mr. Humphrey G. Lunt; Mr Peter J. Henderson and Mr David V. Jones, the author's son.

© Copyright   Westwood Press

November 1986

Printed and Published by The Westwood Press, Print Shop, 44 Boldmere Road Sutton Coldfield, West Midlands. Produced by offset litho.

Contents

Five minutes from Five Ways

Hagley Road, looking towards the City, showing Rotton Park Road on the left, 1923

Priory Road, looking towards Bristol Road, August, 1925

Introduction

EDGBASTON IS A MERE mile from the centre of Birmingham. It is no ordinary suburb. Phrases such as 'a rural oasis', 'an enviable enclave of sylvan beauty', 'the estate with a million trees' and 'Britain's finest 19th century suburb' have been used to describe it.

In view of Edgbaston's close proximity to Birmingham it is not surprising that some of its character has been lost in recent years. Tree-felling for road-widening along the two mile stretch of Hagley Road has reduced the aesthetic appeal of that splendid thoroughfare. Fine period houses have been demolished and large, leafy gardens have been built upon. The needs of commerce and the business world have left their mark, and there has been some high-rise development. Great vigilance and dedication on the part of conservationists will be necessary if irreparable damage is to be avoided to one of the most beautiful suburbs of any English town.

But Edgbaston has more than beauty to commend it. It is a place steeped in history and in this short book I have delved into its colourful past, not forgetting some of the interesting people who have played a part in shaping it.

Douglas V. Jones

Edgbaston Old Church in 1827

Metchley Roman Camp site excavation, 1968

Sir William Dugdale

CHAPTER I

Early History

THE ROMANS MADE a road through the West Midlands and at Metchley Park they built a fort. Edgbaston, however, probably did not exist at that time. The earliest positive information we have is that contained in the Domesday Book of 1086. It was then held in tenure by a man named Drogo. It was rated at two hides, which suggests an area of cultivated land of about 250 acres. It was valued at thirty shillings. The earliest reference to Edgbaston Church is in the 13th century and to the manor-house, known as Edgbaston Hall, somewhat later. Sir William Dugdale in *The Antiquities of Warwickshire,* (1656) relates most of the recorded facts about Edgbaston's early history, intermingled with some speculation.

The name of Edgbaston appears in Domesday as 'Celboldestone', which, Dugdale suggests:

' . . . shews that the denomination of it originally grew from some ancient possessor thereof in the Saxons time.'

Over the centuries the name evolved through various forms, including 'Celbaldston', 'Egbaldeston', and 'Eggebaston' before crystallising into its present form. The suffix 'ton' in the name indicates an Anglo-Saxon settlement and is a common termination for English place names.

Following the Norman Conquest, William Fitz Ausculf at Dudley Castle was the overlord of Edgbaston and many other neighbouring parishes, and Dugdale says:

' . . . one, Drew, held it immediately of him. Whether this Drew was paternal ancestor to Henry, surnamed de Egbaldeston, of whom there is a mention in Henry II's time, I cannot directly affirm, but 'tis likely enough that he might so be, though Henry was the first that I find who assumed it for his surname.'

Edgbaſton.

NOT far from **Erdington, Tame** is enlarged by a Brook called **Rhea,** from the Brittiſh word **Rhe,** [a] **rheawor,** or **rhedeg,** as, I conceive, which ſignifieth to run or flow, and ſeemeth to have its originall from the Greek word *ῥέω fluo:* which torrent hath its riſe from the foot of the **Lickey** hills in **Worceſterſhire,** whence paſſing on with a ſwift courſe, it enters this Countie here at **Edgbaſten,** whereof I am next to take notice. In the Conqueror's Survey [b] this is certified to contain two hides, having Woods that extended to 3. furlongs in length, and half a mile in breadth ; all which were valued at *xxx s.* but there it is written **Celboldeſtone** (which ſhews that the denomination of it originally grew from ſome antient poſſeſſor thereof in the Saxons time) *Will. Fitz Auſculf* (of whom in **Aſton** I have ſpoke) being then the chief Lord of it ; but one *Drew* held it immediatly of him. Whether this *Drew* were paternall anceſtor to *Henry,* ſirnamed *de Egbaldeſton,* of whom there is mention [c] in *H.* 2. time, I cannot directly affirm, but 'tis likely enough that he might ſo be, though *Henry* was the firſt, that I find, who aſſumed it for his ſirname.

From which *Henry* deſcended another *Henry,* who being a Knight [d] in 22. *E.* 1. gave for his Arms, *per pale indented Or and Azure,* as by his Seal [e] and other authorities appeareth. Which Coat hath not onely a reſemblance in the colours, but ſomewhat in the very charge, to the antient Armes of *Bermingham* (as in **Bermingham** may be ſeen) and therefore was doubtleſs aſſumed by the Family of *Eggebaſton,* in imitation of the other, in reſpect of their tenure [f] of this Mannour by military ſervice of the *Berminghams,* who held [g] it over of the Barons of **Dudley.**

The opening passage on Edgbaston in Dugdale's
'The Antiquities of Warwickshire' (1656)

His descendant—another Henry— a knight in the time of Edward I., adopted arms somewhat similar to those of Birmingham. This suggests a subservience to the neighbouring parish, as the de Birminghams were tenants-in-chief and the de Egbaldestons under-tenants of the Barons of Dudley.

Middlemore.

The arms of the Middlemore family topped by 'a moor-cock upon a tuft of reedy grass.'

ARMS.—Quarterly of four. 1 and 4. *Per chevron argent and sable, in chief two moorcocks proper.* 2 and 3. *Per pale indented or and azure.*
CREST.—*In rushes proper a moorcock sitting sable, combed gules.*

There is another possible reason for the similar arms, (heraldic devices), of the two manors. Under a system known as 'Knight's Service', introduced by William I in 1070, every knight had to be available for service for a stipulated number of days each year. In battle conditions the ability to recognise friends and allies depended on being able to understand the involved symbolism of heraldry, emblazoned on the armour of other combatants. The similarity between the coats-of-arms of these two near-neighbours would have facilitated recognition.

To what extent, if any, the de Egbaldestons were involved in military campaigning we do not know, but we do know that later inheritors of the manor were entrusted with what Dugdale called 'sundry great employments', including the raising of armies of foot-soldiers in both Warwickshire and Leicestershire to march against the Scots.

When one, Richard de Egbaldeston, died leaving no male heir, the lordship descended to his daughter, Isabel, and when she married Thomas Middlemore it continued in the possession of that family. It is recorded that this Thomas Middlemore founded the chantry, (a chapel for the chanting of masses), at Studley in the reign of Henry IV. and that he bore for his arms, as Dugdale tells us:

"partie per cheveron argent and sable, two moor-cocks in chief, proper, and for his crest the like moor-cock upon a tuft of reedy grass, as by his seal and the church windows at Studley appeareth."

A later successor to the lordship, Richard Middlemore, having bequeathed his body to be buried in the churchyard at Edgbaston, ordained that six pounds of wax tapers should be burnt about it on the day of the funeral. His widow and executrix, Margerie, thereafter took a vow of chastity and, according to tradition, dedicated herself to improving the fabric of the church. She also directed that, at her own funeral, twenty pounds should be distributed amongst priests, clerks and poor people. Of those poor people themselves we have no record. But we know that throughout the land grinding poverty and hardship was the common lot of the peasantry, and it might be supposed that here at Edgbaston conditions would have been neither better, nor worse, than in other parts of the country.

In the words of one chronicler, Edgbaston Hall echoed to the footsteps of the Middlemores for nearly 300 years. During this time the parish was subjected to the ravages of civil war, which caused great damage to both church and hall.

CHAPTER II

'The Drums and Tramplings
of Conquest'

EDGBASTON AT THE beginning of the seventeenth century was an insignificant place, with only its little church and hall to single it out for distinction. It was sparsely populated, lacked the focal point of a village, and even its church—dedicated to St. Bartholomew but with its origins wrapped in obscurity—was said to have been merely a chapel-of-ease * to the mother-church at Harborne. A place less likely to hear what Sir Thomas Browne called 'the drums and tramplings of conquest' would have been hard to find.

But in 1642 the long-standing differences and hostilities between King Charles I and Parliament erupted into civil war, in which the West Midlands became heavily involved. Allegiances were divided in the region, but in the main sympathies were more with Parliament than with the Royalists. Birmingham was described by Lord Clarendon, author of *The History of the Rebellion in England* as a town of:

'. . . as hearty, wilful, affected disloyalty to the King as any place in England'

and in 1643 Prince Rupert of the Rhine, nephew of Charles I., was sent by the King to punish the town for supplying arms to the Parliamentarians whilst refusing to supply them to the Royalists.

That punishment was severe. The town's defenders, heavily outnumbered by Rupert's troops, were routed. There was killing, burning, robbing and pillaging. According to one contemporary account the Royalist soldiers:

' . . . assaulted many women's chastity, and impudently made their brags of it afterwards . . . That night few or none of them went to bed,

---

* A chapel-of-ease was a place of worship for parishioners living at a distance from their parish-church.

but sat up revelling, robbing and tyrannizing over the poor affrighted women and prisoners, drinking drunk, healthing upon their knees, yea, drinking healths to Prince Rupert's dog'.

The dog, which was called 'Boy' and always accompanied Rupert on his campaigns, was killed at the Battle of Marston Moor in 1644.

Edgbaston Hall during the civil war was the seat of Robert Middlemore, who was both a Royalist supporter and a Roman Catholic. The hall and estate were seized and garrisoned by Parliamentary troops under the command of Colonel John Fox. He made Edgbaston Hall his headquarters and having also taken Hawkesley House on Clent Ridge he used both as bases for raids and onslaughts on surrounding Royalist strongholds. Fox was said to be the son of a tinker from Walsall and the troops under his command had been raised in and around Birmingham. He was known,

A 17th century drawing, commemorating Prince Rupert's presence in the district in 1643

Edgbaston Old Church from an early print

ironically, to his enemies as 'the jovial tinker' on account of his dour countenance. If, as it seems, he was a tinker once removed, it was not unusual for artisans and tradesmen to attain high rank in the Parliamentarian armies.

Both church and hall at Edgbaston were severely damaged during the occupation. The church then was primarily for the use of the lord of the manor and his retainers. Dugdale tells us that within the church were several monuments to the Middlemores, rich in heraldry, but that these had been destroyed at the time he was writing. He concludes by saying:

> *'But of these monuments I might have given a better account had not the church been utterly demolished by the Parliamentary forces in the late wars, when they garrison'd Eggebaston-house'.*

From Dugdale's description it would appear that Fox and his men entirely destroyed the church. They certainly sold the bells, destroyed the monuments, took material from the roof to barricade the hall to make their position more secure and they probably melted down the lead from the roof to make bullets. For a while they also stabled their horses inside the church.

But the greater part of the masonry was left standing, although the upper part of the tower was so much damaged that it had to be rebuilt. For ten years the church apparently lay derelict.

The extent of the damage to the hall by the Parliamentarians is less clear, and in the 1663 Hearth Tax return it was still shown as having 22 hearths. But after the departure of the Parliamentarians it seems that the Middlemores did not re-occupy it and it is recorded that some years later it was totally destroyed. This, it was said, was to prevent its use by Roman Catholics, who were known to be holding services secretly in the parish. The religious intolerance of the time was further emphasised when the Catholics built a chapel in central Birmingham on a site commemorated in the name Masshouse Circus. This was almost immediately destroyed by the Puritans, following which the Catholics rented a house in Pritchatts Road, Edgbaston. There they held their services until 1786, when St. Peter's RC. Chapel was built in St. Peter's Place, off Broad Street, (now demolished).

In 1717, the male line of the Middlemores having been extinguished, the lordship of Edgbaston, then consisting of 1,700 acres, was purchased by Sir Richard Gough from the Middlemore co-heiresses for £20,400. Richard Gough's ancestors were Welsh and had made their money out of wool. He went into industry, travelled in the east, and became a director of the East India Company, following which he was knighted. During ten years at Edgbaston he rebuilt both the church and hall and enclosed the park. When he died in 1727 he was succeeded by his eldest son, Henry, who was created a baronet by George II in 1728.

For his second wife Sir Henry Gough took Barbara Calthorpe, heiress to a number of estates in different parts of the country. From this union was born another Henry,

Sir Richard Gough, who purchased the lordship of Edgbaston in 1717

Idyllic Edgbaston scene by David Cox

who in due course inherited the estates of both his parents. In 1788 the second Sir Henry Gough, in token of having inherited the arms and surname of a family which had become extinct, became Sir Henry Gough-Calthorpe and on his later elevation to the peerage, Baron Calthorpe of Calthorpe in the County of Norfolk.

No member of the Calthorpe family has occupied Edgbaston Hall since 1783, but despite their absence the estate has continued in their ownership to this day with every possible opportunity having been taken in earlier times to increase its size on favourable terms without losing its character in the face of the rising tide of Birmingham's growth.

Toll-house and gate at Five Ways, c. 1800

Sketch made near Five Ways Gate   *(H.H. Lines)*

CHAPTER III

The 18th Century Scene

THE YEAR AFTER Sir Richard Gough's purchase of the lordship of Edgbaston saw the appearance of a survey from which we get a glimpse of the parish as it was early in the 18th century. This survey was made by a man named Sparry in 1718. It portrays Edgbaston as a tiny scattered hamlet, lacking a village centre, with sixty-four houses spread over a wide area.

At that time the road from Birmingham to Bromsgrove and Worcester was by way of Edgbaston Street, which as far back as King John's reign was known a 'Egebaston Strete', the word 'strete' denoting a paved way in a town. Thence the traveller in former times would have followed a route marked today by Smallbrook Ringway, Holloway Head, Bath Row, Wheeley's Road, Arthur Road, Church Road and to a point half-way down Priory Road, where the road then divided. The left-hand fork led to Edgbaston Mill and Moseley and the right fork cut across the lower end of Edgbaston Park, crossed the brook below Edgbaston Pool and joined the course of the present Bristol Road at Bourne Brook.

The making of turnpike roads in the 18th century entailed the building of toll-houses and gates. In Edgbaston these were located on the old road, near the entrance to Edgbaston Hall and at the Five Ways end of Islington Row. There was also one round the corner at the top end of Broad Street, which marked the boundary between Birmingham and Edgbaston, and a further one at the junction of Hagley Road and Sandon Road, then called Smethwick Lane.

In 1771 a new section of turnpike road was made, starting at Bristol Street, then called Exeter Row. It joined the old road near the Gun Barrels Inn. That part of the old road across Edgbaston Park was then abandoned and a new toll-gate was erected at Edgbaston Lane, (now Edgbaston Road). Pershore Road was cut early in the 19th century, when a toll-house and gate were erected near the Pebble Mill.

Toll Gate, Pershore Road near Pebble Mill

(Charles F. Barwell)

Parish boundaries were marked by boundary stones. Until recent years there was one such boundary stone set into the old bridge, (now demolished), in Belgrave Road, spanning the River Rea. This marked the old boundary between the parishes of Edgbaston and Kings Norton, which was once a much larger parish than it is today.

From Sparry and other sources a composite picture of Edgbaston two centuries ago emerges. Near the entrance to Edgbaston Hall, close by the church, was the parish pound, or pinfold, an enclosure where stray animals were confined. It was moved twice, once to the corner of Hagley Road and Plough and Harrow Road and, later, to near the White Swan Inn at the bottom of Chad Hill. Church Road was a narrow lane and beside it—opposite the Hall—was an avenue of beech trees, known as 'the Grove', planted, it is believed, to shelter the Hall from north-east winds.

The Over Mill, c. 1962

The remains of Over Mill in 1986

Many of the modern thoroughfares we know now were rough tracks, country lanes and sometimes merely field paths. Hagley Road was known as Grindlestone Lane and Harborne Road was called Long Lane or, alternatively, Green Lane. Richmond Hill Road was described as being one of the prettiest lanes in the district, with a farmhouse fronted by a duck-pond and backed by a row of ricks. The site of present-day Brook Road was then called Snailes Green and at the bottom of Chad Hill, on Harborne Road, there was a group of cottages, known as Good Knaves End. Nearby lived Joseph Smith, a renowned bell-founder, whose name has been recorded on a large number of church bells in the Midlands, dated between 1701 and 1732.

Chad Hill was sometimes known as Hungry Hill and nearby was a farm of 88 acres with its farmhouse situated opposite the present entrance to the Botanical Gardens in Westbourne Road. This farm did not come into the

Pen and ink drawing of Speedwell Mill in the 19th century

Edgbaston Mill and mill-house in 1898

The same site in 1986, showing the surviving mill-house, now occupied by the
Tally Ho Tennis Club

Rear view of Edgbaston Mill and mill-house in 1898

possession of the Calthorpe family until 1820. In addition to the old road between Birmingham and Edgbaston, there was a footpath across fields between the two places, known as Speaking Stile Walk. Philip B. Chatwin in his *A History of Edgbaston,* writing in 1914, relates that, at that time, a short length of the walk, opposite St. Thomas's Church, Holloway Head still retained the old name.

There were formerly several water-mills in the district. Over Mill on Chad Brook, just south of Edgbaston Pool in the grounds of Edgbaston Golf Course was once a blade-mill. Edgbaston Mill, a corn-mill, was on the River Rea and situated on the site of Tally Ho Tennis Club in Edgbaston Road, where the manorial millhouse still survives. Speedwell Mill, also on the Rea, was a rolling-mill; Princess Road was made over the site of its filled in mill-pond. A fourth mill, Pebble Mill, on the Bourn Brook, was successively a fulling-mill,* a blade-mill and a corn-mill. The site is now occupied by the Midland Headquarters of the B.B.C.

---

* A fulling-mill is one in which woollen-cloth is 'fulled' or cleansed.

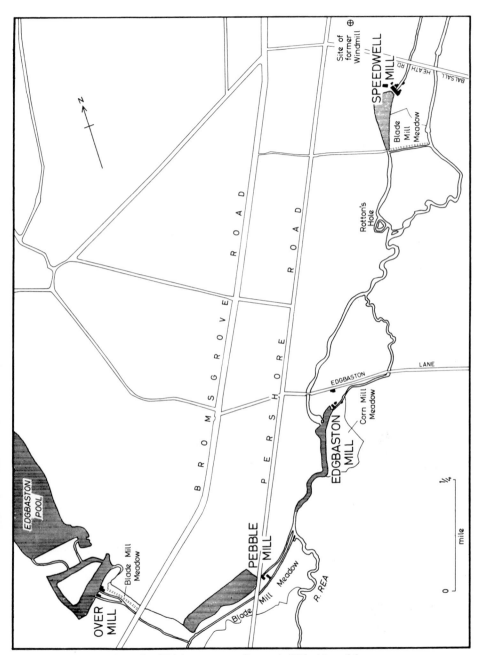

*The Mills of Edgbaston, according to the Tithe Map of the
Parish of Edgbaston, 1843*

23

Edgbaston mill-house and its garden, (see also page 21)

Edgbaston Lane, showing bridge over the River Rea

Law and order were enforced by one parish constable. In the 1730s an elderly man named Moss was said to have held the post, who wore in his official capacity a long blue coat with a red collar. Watchmen with lanterns and rattles patrolled the roads at night, proclaiming the hour and the state of the weather.

What of Birmingham itself two-and-a-half centuries ago? The view from Highgate would have been of a town whose houses had large, well-cultivated gardens. Easy Row was a beautiful suburb, at the end of which was John Baskerville's house and printing works set in seven acres of pasturage and garden. New Hall stood amid its extensive parkland, spanning an area from Colmore Row to Newhall Hill and Frederick Street in the jewellery district.

In the valley below Carrs Lane were meadows and trees forming the park of the de Bermingham family, commemorated in the names of Park Street and Little Park Street. Below St. Martin's Church was the parsonage and the moat which once surrounded the de Bermingham's castle. Nearby was the Lady Well, the pure water of which was conveyed to various parts of the town in a large cask or hogshead on wheels, drawn by a horse.

But the scene was soon to be transformed, due in no small measure to those two 'harbingers of the Industrial Revolution', James Watt and Matthew Boulton. Watt had a patent for a static steam engine and Boulton had the capital and know-how to develop it. Between them they overcame Birmingham's inadequacy in water power, necessary for operating its mills and forges at a time of increasing industrial growth. At their Soho Foundry both men made vast fortunes and the ensuing prosperity brought to the town resulted in a huge increase of population and many great changes in its physical appearance.

Doctor William Withering, whose book, 'An Account of the Foxglove' made medical history

A N

A C C O U N T

OF THE

F O X G L O V E,

A N D

Some of its Medical Ufes:

W I T H

PRACTICAL REMARKS ON DROPSY,

AND OTHER DISEASES.

B Y

WILLIAM WITHERING, M. D.

Phyfician to the General Hofpital at Birmingham.

—— *a non-pu premator in annum.*

HORACE.

BIRMINGHAM: PRINTED BY M. SWINNEY:

FOR

G. G. J. AND J. ROBINSON, PATERNOSTER-ROW, LONDON

M.DCC.LXXXV.

26

CHAPTER IV

Luminaries and Looters

OF ALL THE tenants who were to occupy Edgbaston Hall after the departure of the Calthorpes, none is better known to posterity than Dr. William Withering, who came to live there in 1786. His fame rests largely on his having discovered the medical uses of the foxglove (digitalis) in the treatment of heart disease. On this subject he wrote an important treatise for which he was made a Fellow of the Royal Society. He is also remembered for his part in founding the Birmingham General Hospital and for having written a book on scarlet-fever and a botany in two volumes. When he moved to Edgbaston Hall the learned doctor could not have anticipated the nature of the troubles he would encounter a few years later.

Dr. Withering became a member of the Birmingham-based Lunar Society, consisting of a dozen or so eminent men, including James Watt, Matthew Boulton, Josiah Wedgwood, the potter, Dr Joseph Priestley, scientist and dissenting minister, and Thomas Day, writer and disciple of Rousseau. Informal meetings were held at members' houses and dinner, accompanied by a bottle or two of wine, preceded a discussion of their wide-ranging scientific and philosophical interests. The name Lunar Society was chosen because its members met once a month on the Sunday nearest the time of the full moon so as to have its light by which to return home along unlit roads. Perhaps not without a trace of acrimony on the part of their less intellectually endowed contemporaries, members of the Lunar Society came to be known as 'lunatics'.

But in 1791 derision changed to anger. Many intellectuals, including Priestley, had acclaimed the French Revolution, believing it to be a herald of universal liberty and brotherhood. A dinner was held in Birmingham to commemorate the second anniversary of the burning of the Bastille in 1789. This provoked a mob reaction. Rioters and looters went on the rampage to the cry of 'No philosophers—Church and King for ever!' The homes of radicals, dissenters and intellectuals were pillaged and burnt. Priestley's Sparkhill home, among others, was fired, together with his laboratory,

Old print depicting the Birmingham Riots of 1791

books and scientific papers, despite the fact that he had not been present at the dinner. He became a refugee, fleeing first to Sutton Coldfield before going further afield and eventually leaving England permanently for America.

Edgbaston Hall and Pool

A great deal of property had been destroyed before the rioters set their sights on Edgbaston Hall, by which time the military had been sent for. We have a graphic account of the events of July, 1791 from the pen of none other than Dr. Withering himself in a letter to his landlord, Sir Henry Gough-Calthorpe. Having said in it that his gardener had found out that an attack on the Hall was imminent, the Doctor continued:

"On Saturday morning, about ten o'clock he brought me positive information that Edgbaston Hall would be burnt down on Sunday night. I immediately set about the necessary preparation; removed three cart and wagon loads of the most valuable property; but about two o'clock of the same day I found that a plundering party of about 300 were coming upon us from Ladywood. Part of them stop'd at Westley's house, and 250 reached us before the second wagon could get away, which was therefore driven into the hay-field and covered with hay. This party of plunderers had regularly preceded the other larger and more determined incendiaries. Twenty guineas and drink had bribed them from Ladywood. By treating and bribing we also got shut of them . . . Before night the house was completely stripped, both of furniture and fixtures, most of which were deposited in the church and

guarded by some of our best men . . . About eight o'clock this evening, the dreaded incendiaries arrived to the amount of near 30. I was in Birmingham, expecting the arrival of the military every hour, and every half-hour accounts came to town that the hall was actually in flames, but the zeal and activity of a few friends who had courage to act suspended its fate.''

Bribes, free drinks and persuasion got most of the mob to adjourn to an inn to spend two guineas. The more determined of the looters were attacked by Dr. Withering's friends and supporters, when one of the two ringleaders was reported to have been 'left for dead' and the other severely beaten. After some heavy fighting the rest of the hard-core looters were routed by the Hall's defenders.

The arrival of the military in Birmingham saw the end of the riots. Peace was restored and, according to one commentator, 'the grimy contingent found it wisest to retire with as good grace as might be, to their own regions'. During the next few years, Dr. Withering's health declined and he died in 1799, aged 58. He was buried in a vault in Edgbaston Church and his monument there has a lament in verse. Not surprisingly, the foxglove and the healing serpent feature in the carved stonework, a tribute both to Dr. Withering and to eighteenth century lapidary art.

Dr. Joseph Priestley's house at Sparkhill after having been pillaged and burnt by rioters in 1791

CHAPTER V

The Age of Elegance

THE RESIDENTIAL development of Edgbaston began early in the 19th century with the building of houses to cater for the needs of Birmingham's more prosperous inhabitants. Many of the town's manufacturers and entrepreneurs, having lived close to, or in some cases, above their workshops or factories, on becoming more successful, moved out to the Five Ways area. The appeal was that of moving from the town into the country, with unbroken rural vistas extending to Harborne and Moseley. To accommodate these *nouveaux riches* many of the Calthorpe estate tenant farmers were ousted, although for many years Edgbaston remained predominantly farm-land. As late as 1891 there were still 1,113 acres of agricultural land in the parish.

The century prior to the outbreak of war in 1914 was one of continuous growth in Edgbaston, though with some fluctuations in the rate. Birmingham in the same period was expanding hugely to accommodate its vast new army of factory workers, many of whom lived in mean and insanitary back-to-back houses. But in Edgbaston speculative building was excluded and widely spaced houses, set in big gardens, were the norm. It was a salubrious place in every way, its air was clean and invigorating and its soil light and well-drained. In the late 19th century the average annual death rate per thousand was 11.8, whereas in Birmingham it was 21.4.

Many new roads were cut, most of them named after various members of the Calthorpe family. The creation of a turnpike road from Birmingham to Pershore early in the 19th century opened up a new area for development. Some good-quality working class homes were built, notably in the Sun Street, Spring Street and Balsall Heath Road areas and later, in Varna Road and Princess Road. Many fine houses were built along Hagley Road and Bristol Road to serve the needs of the well-to-do. By 1863 there were large residences on both sides of Hagley Road, extending from Five Ways to Portland Road. The advent of public transport further increased the building tempo.

ELEGANT EDGBASTON

Joseph Chamberlain was Mayor of Birmingham between 1873 and 1876 and his municipal achievements during that period were largely responsible for earning Birmingham its epithet of 'the best governed city in the world'. The spin-off was a demand for even more leases for homes in Edgbaston, (all buildings on the Calthorpe estate were then leasehold). The population there increased from 9,269 in 1851 to 22,760 in 1881.

In time Edgbaston became less exclusive. Some 'zoning' took place, segregating the homes of the rich from those of the comfortably well-off middle classes and the more successful artisans who came to live there. Generation by generation the Calthorpes kept a tight rein on developments, always with what they saw as the best interests of the estate at heart.

Two of those 19th century Calthorpes are worthy of mention, if only for their contrasting characters. George, the third Lord Calthorpe, who held the title from 1807 to 1851, despite being somewhat of an entrepreneur, was a man of liberal views, an advocate of parliamentary reform, an opponent

Georgian terrace in Hagley Road

of slavery and a close friend of William Wilberforce, who did so much in the cause of emancipating slaves. Frederick Henry William, the fifth Lord Calthorpe, title holder from 1868 to 1893, was a bachelor-playboy, friend of the Prince of Wales, a big spender with a mistress in Paris, yet described as 'a man at ease in the world of high finance'.

It was made clear to the working class immigrants to the Calthorpe estate that there should be no trade or manufacturing on the estate, and that there should be 'no shops, work-shops, ale-houses, brew shops, tea gardens or public strawberry-gardens'. It was further ordained that there should be 'no erection or building whatsoever which shall or may be deemed a nuisance or otherwise injurious to the said Lord Calthorpe'. A variety of proposals were successfully opposed, including those for a public urinal at the junction of Pershore Road and Speedwell Road and a fried fish-shop in Varna Road, its proposed site described as being 'within sniffing distance of some of Edgbaston's most palatial mansions.' Tenants were often supportive of these exclusions, believing them to be in the cause of maintaining the value of their homes.

The Round House, St James's Road

Cottages in Hermitage Road

Botanical Gardens, Birmingham

A sense of community was engendered by a monthly periodical, the *Edgbastonia,* founded in 1881, 3,000 copies of which were distributed, free, to householders. It consisted of features and news items of local interest, and was claimed to be 'free from political or sectarian bias.' Its revenue came from advertising.

From time to time consessions were made by the Calthorpes, enabling a number of institutes to be established on the estate. These included, in the 19th century, the Deaf and Dumb Institute and the Blind Institute, the Oratory and the Oratory School and land for Warwickshire County Cricket Club, soon to become one of the most highly regarded county cricket grounds in the country. In the same era the Birmingham Botanical and Horticultural Society acquired a lease on land off Westbourne Road, known as 'Holly Bank.' The site was laid out by John Claudius Loudon, a prominent landscape gardener and architect. Loudon, an unworldly man, described as 'a Scot without business instincts', with his wife, Jane, spent six weeks on the Edgbaston project, but he asked for no fee and was, as a consequence, paid only his expenses for the visit.

Jane Loudon, a native of Birmingham, was a woman of diverse talents, who wrote a futuristic novel at 20, entitled 'The Mummy', in which she envisaged life in the year 2126. Her vision was of air travel in huge balloons; a rocket postal service; empty prisons and by means of electricity the ability to draw down rain in times of drought. Her subsequent interest in gardening, kindled by her husband, led to her writing a book, *Gardening for Ladies,* and many other books on kindred subjects.

The ten enchanted acres of the Botanical Gardens were first opened to shareholders of the Society in June, 1832. The general public at that time had no access, but changes were soon to be made. Tickets of admission were granted in the first instance to the colonel and officers of the Scots Greys,

The ten enchanted acres of the Botanical Gardens were first opened
in June, 1832

THE RHODODENDRON GARDEN   THE BOTANICAL GARDENS, EDGBASTON

THE ALPINE GARDEN   THE BOTANICAL GARDENS, EDGBASTON

quartered in the town, and, at Easter, 1838 non-shareholders were admitted on payment of one shilling—a charge which, at that time, would have been prohibitive to the poor.

In 1844 the Society first permitted the gardens, but not the greenhouses, to be opened on Mondays to what was termed 'bona fide members of the working class'. No baskets or hoops were permitted, smoking was forbidden and two policemen were there to keep order. The charge was one penny. The choice of a weekday, it must be assumed, would have limited the number of workers attending at any one time.

Herbert Morrison, the then Deputy Prime Minister, throwing at a coconut at the Labour Party Gala, Botanical Gardens, 1948

'Church on Sunday'   *Drawn by Charles Radclyffe*

Edgbaston in 1837, the site of Wellington Road   *Drawn by Samuel Line*

SERIOUS ACCIDENT AT BIRMINGHAM.

BURSTING OF THE CANAL AT EDGBASTON,
On Sunday Morning, May 26th, 1872.

Commemorating an event which caused considerable damage to homes and gardens in Gough Road, Pakenham Road and Charlotte Road

Edgbaston Hall, 1891

Hagley Road, Monument Road junction
(J. Burgoyne)

A quiet corner of Edgbaston Park

CHAPTER VI

The 'Harborne Express' v. the Horse-'bus and the Tramcar

THE EIGHTEENTH CENTURY saw the beginning of those great social and industrial changes which we call the Industrial Revolution. This involved a mass migration of workers from the country to the towns for work in the factories. Communications were improved in the course of the century by the making of turnpike roads and canals, and many towns grew massively.

Burgeoning industry in Birmingham, with no navigable river within twenty miles, made the need for improved roads imperative. Turnpike trusts were formed and toll-gates erected to collect tolls from travellers to pay for road improvements. There were several toll-gates in Edgbaston, (see Chapter III).

Canals were hardly less important than roads for accommodating Birmingham's needs. In 1791 an act of parliament was passed, authorising the construction of a canal from Birmingham to Worcester, which entailed its passing through the Edgbaston estate. Sir Henry Gough-Calthorpe was a shareholder in the construction company, and he was able to obtain clauses in the act, prohibiting the building of factories, workshops or warehouses along the canal in Edgbaston. No reservoirs were to be made in the vicinity and the towpath was to be on the opposite side to that of the hall. These protective clauses have proved to be most effective. That stretch of the canal through Edgbaston has retained its semi-rural image to this day—a fact which can be illustrated by travelling on the cross-city line, south, from New Street Station.

The need for a local canal feeder reservoir was met in 1825, when Thomas Telford commenced the construction of one in the Rotton Park valley, on the site of Roach Pool. Rotton Park Reservoir was completed in 1827, and in 1870 it was described as being "the finest sheet of water in the midland counties."

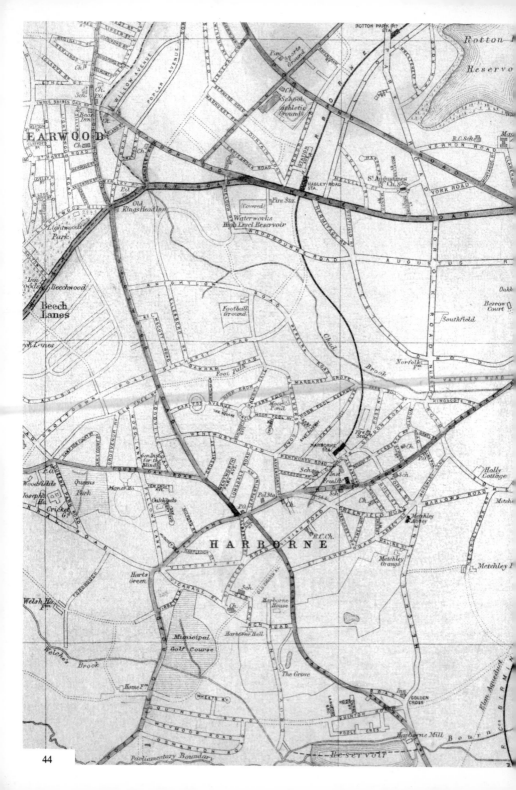

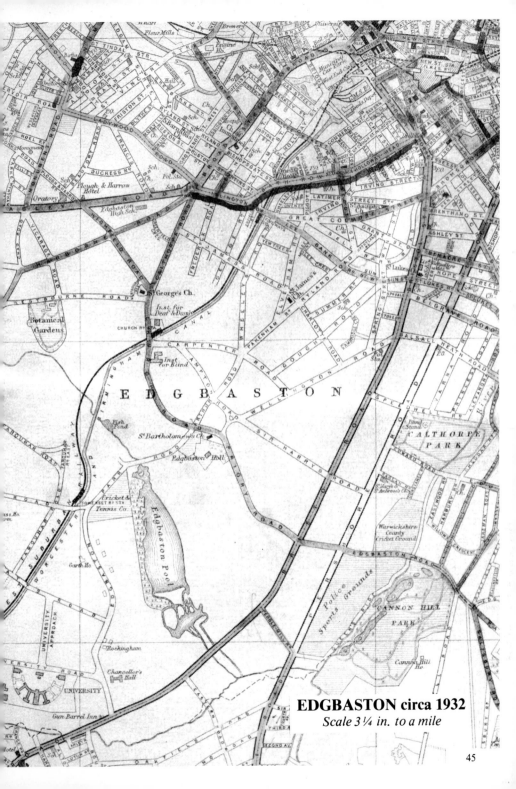

EDGBASTON circa 1932
Scale 3 ¼ in. to a mile

45

The 'Harborne Express' passing through Hagley Road cutting under a
full head of steam   *(Harborne Library)*

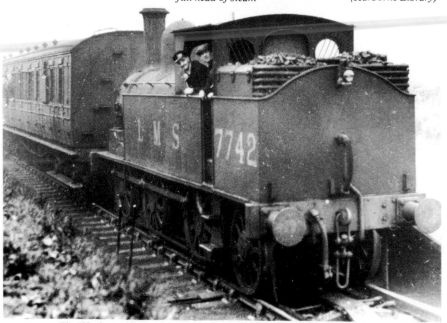

The 'Harborne Express' at Hagley Road Station on 24th November, 1934
(W.A. Camwell)

During the 19th century Birmingham's suburbs proliferated. Edgbaston was becoming encircled by the rapidly growing communities of Harborne, Moseley, Bearwood, Selly Oak and Bournbrook. Its rural vistas were fast diminishing. By 1846 six horse-'buses were operating daily in each direction along both Hagley Road and Bristol Road, with five to and from Harborne. A quarter of a century later three different companies were operating half-hourly horse-'bus services on all the main roads through Edgbaston, incuding the Pershore Road.

In the same period a network of trunk railways was being built, criss-crossing the country, and in 1838 Birmingham was linked by rail with London. But it was not until later in the century that many branch railway lines were made to cater for the needs of an ever more mobile society. In 1866 a bill was promoted in parliament for the building of a railway between New Street Station and Harborne, running on single track from where it left the main line near Monument Lane and with intermediate stations at Icknield Port Road, Rotton Park Road and Hagley Road, (near Gillott Road). The Harborne Railway was an independent company, but was operated by the London and North Western Railway Company until 1923, when it became a part of the London, Midland and Scottish Railway Company. It was opened to traffic in 1874.

Two years later the Midland Railway Company opened a line from Birmingham to Kings Norton, with stations at Five Ways, Church Road and Somerset Road to serve the needs of Edgbastonians. This line was made parallel with the Worcester Canal and later became part of the main line to Bristol. It also now incorporates the cross-city line between Four Oaks and Longbridge. Church Road and Somerset Road stations no longer exist, but a new station to serve the needs of the University was opened in May, 1978, coinciding with the commencement of the cross-city service.

The Harborne Railway became known affectionately as 'The Harborne Express' and was a legend in its own lifetime. The service was operated by little 2-4-2 tankers and the running time for the uphill journey from New Street to Harborne was 22 minutes and for the return trip, 18 minutes. Although time-keeping was good. the slowness of the service led to many jokes. You could, it was said, pick flowers on the way. Comic postcards were produced, one of which depicted a man with a red flag walking in front of the engine and with a trackside notice reading 'Season-tickets for a single journey'.

The Harborne Railway Company originally operated a reduced service on Sundays, but this was soon abandoned, due to objections by Hagley Road

The abandoned route of the 'Harborne Express', c. 1970

residents over the disturbance of the Sabbath peace and quiet. The line was closed to passenger traffic in November, 1934, not without some nostalgia. Extra coaches had to be added for the last journey from New Street to Harborne, and as reported in the local press, the 'Harborne Express' was not allowed to pass out of existence 'unwept, unhonoured and unsung.'

The line remained open to freight trains until 1963, which enabled the Stephenson Locomotive Society to run a special steam train over the track in 1950 for the benefit of enthusiasts, and another one in November, 1963 before final closure of the line. The route of the old Harborne Railway is now a peaceful, two-mile 'Walkway', given over to dog-walkers and nature lovers.

The need for road passenger transport continued to grow. Both Hagley Road and Bristol Road became busier and early in the present century the increasing number of horse 'buses were augmented by motor 'buses. Bristol Road was also served by horse trams, later converted to steam trams and then to a battery-operated electric tramway. Despite strong local opposition to trams, this apparently caused little resentment as Bristol Road was near the boundary of the estate and was less prestigious than Hagley Road.

Motor 'buses, it was said, were only welcomed by the residents of Hagley Road as an alternative to trams, but they were not popular. There were a number of accidents involving runaway motor 'buses, including one which hit a garden wall in Hagley Road. They were also found to have difficulty in ascending Harborne Hill, and in October, 1907 the *Birmingham Daily Post* carried the following item:

EXIT THE MOTOR 'BUS

After tomorrow night there will be no such thing as a motor omnibus in Birmingham. The last motor omnibus will run its course on Saturday night, and then its work, so far as Birmingham is concerned, will be done. . .

The services reverted to horse-'buses.

Under the Birmingham Corporation Act of 1903 a municipal tramways committee was formed and the following year the first ten Corporation electric tramcars went into service between Steelhouse Lane and Aston. Apart from this service, road passenger transport at that time consisted of privately operated steam trams, horse trams, cable cars and horse 'buses. But at the beginning of 1907 Birmingham Corporation put 200 new electric tramcars onto the streets of the city, and many of the old conveyances were relegated to the scrap-heap.

The threat of trams along Hagley Road loomed large. Opposition stiffened and Lord Calthorpe made his views known. Trams, he said, would detract from the quiet of Edgbaston and reduce the value of property. Tenants supported him almost to a man, and the feared event was, for a time, postponed. But in 1912 parliament enacted a bill giving Birmingham

The coming of the tramcar was a great affront to the inhabitants of Edgbaston

Tiller-steered car outside the Plough and Harrow Hotel, c. 1900

Corporation the authority to build a tramway from Birmingham by way of Holloway Head, Bath Row and Islington Row to Five Ways, then along Hagley Road to the 'King's Head' at the junction of Lordswood Road and Bearwood Road. The service came into operation in September, 1913.

The electric tramcar was a cheap and, in its day, an efficient means of transport, but it was always seen as a conveyance for the working classes, its presence tending to give a down-market image to those places it traversed. It is doubtful whether Edgbastonians ever really came to terms with having trams running along Hagley Road, and the route was one of the first in Birmingham to change over to 'buses in 1930.

Five Ways snow scene, February, 1909 (Dr. J. Hall Edwards)

THE MANY FACES OF FIVE WAYS

988. AT FIVE WAYS. BIRMINGHAM

FIVE WAYS   BIRMINGHAM.

52

FIVE WAYS. EDGBASTON. A.   10.

54

Edgbaston Hall, now the club house of Edgbaston Golf Club

A surviving memento of the Second World War over the cellar door of Edgbaston Hall

*'Edgbaston Golf Course is one of the finest in the country, set amidst
beautiful surroundings'*

A morning mist over Edgbaston Golf Course, photographed from the Hall

The Impact of the 20th Century

EDGBASTON AT THE turn of the century was a quiet, semi-rural, up-market residential area. It was characterised by large, Georgian, Regency and Victorian houses, set in acres of gardens. Hagley Road, that most splendid of thoroughfares, rang to the clip-clopping of horses' hooves and the rattling and rumbling of the horse-'buses, their steady 5-10 mph. sometimes reduced on account of a flock of sheep, being driven along the road to market.

Even as late as the 1920s it was possible to see, from gardens in Wellington Road, green fields and grazing sheep on the far side of Bristol Road. Farm-land for long survived around the estate, and due to a slump in late Victorian times, some of the new roads had empty plots for many years. One of the last major roads to be cut was Barnsley Road in 1901, linking Hagley Road with Sandon Road.

The coming of the motor-car gave greater mobility to well-to-do Edgbastonians, some of whom, to avoid increasing urbanisation, moved further afield, to such deeply rural places as Knowle and Solihull then were. This fact may have been responsible for temporarily retarding Edgbaston's growth early in the century.

When Mason College in Edmund Street, Birmingham, (founded by Josiah Mason in 1870), was converted into a university, Joseph Chamberlain became its first chancellor in 1900. Following a request by him for land on the Calthorpe estate for a new university building at Bournbrook, 25 acres were given for that purpose. It was stipulated, however, that there must be no houses, pubs, smoke, fumes or smells and that the structure should be used 'solely for the purpose of a university for ever.' The new building, dominated by its 325 feet Chamberlain Clock Tower, was completed in 1909, and opened amid great jubilation by King Edward VII on 7th July of that year.

Birmingham University under construction, 1908
(Benjamin Stone)

Joseph Chamberlain, Statesman and first Chancellor of Birmingham University

A post-card commemorating the opening of Birmingham University
by King Edward VII in 1909

The varying fortunes of any family often lead to a situation where no male heir exists to inherit the estate. Such was the case in 1910 when Augustus, the sixth Lord Calthorpe, died. His only son, Walter, had died four years earlier and the Edgbaston estate passed to Rachel, the eldest of his four daughters. At the same time the peerage passed to Augustus's brother, together with the Perry Hall estate, which was later sold to Birmingham Corporation and made into a public park.

Rachel, having married Fitzroy Hamilton Lloyd-Anstruther, added the name Anstruther to that of her own, which accounts for the double-hyphenated 'Anstruther-Gough-Calthorpe', still used by the family. Rachel died in the early 'fifties and her husband a few years later, he by that time having been created a baronet. The succession of their eldest son and heir, Sir Richard Hamilton Anstruther-Gough-Calthorpe was curious in that he inherited the Edgbaston estate from his mother and his title from his father. When he died in 1985 he was succeeded by his grandson, Euan, who was eighteen at the time and became the third baronet, Euan's father, Niall, having been killed in a road accident in 1971.

The University, Birmingham.

When the Great War broke out in August, 1914, there was a great rush to the colours, and in Edgbaston, as in most other places, there was an exodus of the young, able-bodied men of the parish. Belgian refugees were accommodated in Hagley Road, charitable fund-raising events were organised and school-girls ran 'knitting parties' to make comforts for the troops.

There were the customary dismal lists of casualties, and a reminder appeared in *Edgbastonia* in December, 1915:

'Edgbastonia' would be obliged if relatives of Edgbastonians who fall in the service of their country would forward with the intimation of death a photograph and any biographical details in their possession.'

The new university was converted into a military hospital, and the wounded de-trained at nearby Selly Oak Station. A shortage of ambulances for stretcher cases was counteracted by an enterprising Edgbastonian, Mr E.M. Tailby, who designed a two-wheeled covered trailer-ambulance at a cost of £35 for hitching by tow-bar to a motor-car. There was a good

BIRMINGHAM UNIVERSITY AS A MILITARY HOSPITAL

All photos by Bernard Moore

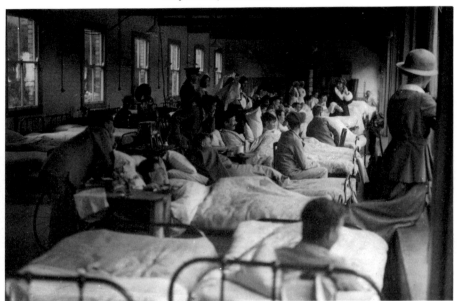

*Wounded soldiers watching a production of 'Twelth Night' by
Birmingham Repertory Company*

St. Johns nurses on the way to Hospital Memorial service to Lord Kitchener, 1916

Hospital tents outside University

Transporting the wounded by double-decker ambulance

response to an appeal for funds and several of the trailers were added to the fleet of ambulances. There was an equally good response to an appeal for volunteers to have tow-bars fitted to their cars.

The era of peace between 1918 and 1939 saw few changes in Edgbaston and it continued to maintain its élitist image. New circular 'bus routes were inaugurated, which passed through the estate, the Outer Circle in 1926 and the Inner Circle in 1928. A few blocks of flats, forerunners of the high-rise buildings which were later to darken the skyline, made their appearance. One such was Viceroy Close, the block of luxury flats in Bristol Road, built in the late 'thirties in a style typical of the period. Over each of 15 front doors leading to the flats are curious, carved mask-faces by Oliver O'Connor Barrett, which give added interest to the building.

Following the death in 1927 of Sir Henry Barber, a benefactor of the university, a trust was set up and the Barber Institute of Fine Arts was formed. On a site adjacent to the University, picture galleries and a hall for musical recitals were provided, and the late Dr. Thomas Bodkin was appointed as the first Barber Professor of Fine Arts. It was Professor Bodkin who acquired the early 18th century bronze equestrian statue of George I. in Dublin in 1937, which now stands beside the entrance to the University in Edgbaston Park Road. He bought it for the knock-down price of £500.

The last private tenant of Edgbaston Hall was Sir James Smith, the first lord mayor of Birmingham,* who lived there from 1908 until his death in 1932. The lease then reverted to the Calthorpe Estate and in 1936 it was granted to Edgbaston Golf Club, when they moved there from Warley. Within the grounds the mixed woodland, together with Edgbaston Pool, still provide sanctuary for much wild life, and at the southern end of the pool can be seen the remains of the old blade-mill, long since defunct.

The early 18th century bronze equestrian statue of George I which stands beside the entrance to the University in Edgbaston Park Road

---

* *His predecessors only held the title of 'Mayor'.*

The Campus, Birmingham University, 1986

Following the closure of the King Edward VI School in New Street, Birmingham, prior to demolition, the school moved to its present site in Edgbaston Park Road in 1938 and in the same year, on 14th July, the Queen Elizabeth Hospital was formally opened. Subsequent expansion of both the hospital and the university in the Metchley Park area has almost obliterated the site of the Roman fort there, built in AD.46, when the legions were advancing into the Midlands. It is said to have assumed some importance during Boadicea's revolt against the conquerors in AD.60.

The war of 1939-1945 brought a new frightfulness with the large-scale involvement of the civilian population, due to aerial bombardment. Even as early as 1939 the Germans had plans for the destruction of a number of industrial sites in Birmingham. If Edgbaston suffered less than some other suburbs it may have been due to the lack of such targets within its boundaries. There was, however, one minor war-time industrial incursion—a button-factory in a house in Carpenter Road.

There was some damage to property. Homes were devastated on the estate's perimeter and at Viceroy Close there was a 'near miss' when a bomb

House in Calthorpe Road, the home of John Cadbury for 35 years

fell in the drive, making a large crater and hurling a block of concrete through the roof of one of the flats. Several bombs were said to have fallen harmlessly on the golf course where, as part of the war effort, farmers were allowed to graze their sheep and grow potatoes. Over the fifteenth fairway flew a barrage-balloon, while in Edgbaston Hall the cellar was reinforced and made proof against poison-gas.

For some years after the war ended in 1945, Edgbaston changed little. In 1947 Birmingham Corporation initiated a development plan for the city and at that time the general concensus of opinion was that the exclusive character of the Calthorpe Estate should be maintained. Edgbaston, it was thought, set a standard of excellence and was a model to inspire future planners. By 1950 houses there still did not exceed 1.5 to the acre. In that year, however, the Calthorpe Estate agreed to sell four 'fringe areas', amounting to about 100 acres, to Birmingham Corporation for housing redevelopment. These were the least pleasing parts of the estate, ripe for redevelopment, with little aesthetic appeal, and the arrangement was considered to be advantageous to both parties.

Church of the Redeemer, Hagley Road, Wyndham Road junction
(now demolished)

In 1957 a local architect, John Madin, was commissioned to make proposals for the redevelopment of the Calthorpe Estate and to act as consulting architect. By then it had already been accepted that there should be 'commercial zoning' around Five Ways. Some houses there were already in use as offices of firms bombed out of their city premises during the war. Other firms had merely moved there from a high-risk area. John Madin's plan was formulated and published the following year and has been the basis of Edgbaston's subsequent redevelopment.

Vast changes occurred all around Edgbaston. Some high-rise flats were built to achieve the required greater density of population. Many large houses were demolished and small, select estates were built on their sites and in the spacious gardens in which they stood. Between 1961 and 1967 some 1,500 houses were built on the Calthorpe Estate. Large houses along Hagley Road were converted into hotels, restaurants, offices and consulting-rooms. Approval was given in 1966 for the making of the Five Ways underpass. Large scale demolition ensued, which included that of King Edward's Grammar School, Five Ways. When completed, the underpass transformed the character and appearance of that ancient road junction, first referred to in the 16th century as 'Fyve Wayes.'

The last twenty years have seen a continuation of the planned regeneration of Edgbaston and the disappearance of much old property. Many of the demolished Victorian mansions were said by the Calthorpe Estate office to have been 'both physically and socially obsolete.' The result, as they proclaim in their booklet, *Edgbaston—where the trees begin:*

'. . . *is a balanced community for which a vast range of accommodation is available—be it for the young first time buyers; the senior executive and his family; or those who have retired and whose families have grown up. The one common feature which is equally available to all, however, is the unique setting of Edgbaston.*'

Present-day Edgbaston has much of interest and enjoyment for both tourists and local people. Edgbaston Old Church embodies an amalgam of styles, the oldest being probably late fifteenth or early sixteenth century, and despite the accretions of later periods it still has the outward appearance of a medieval, sandstone parish church. The splendid eighteenth century Edgbaston Hall, replacing an earlier structure, includes alterations made in 1852 by Sir Charles Barry, architect of the Houses of Parliament. The Oratory in Hagley Road was established by Cardinal John Henry Newman in 1852 and the Oratory School seven years later, where the distinguished writer, Hilaire Belloc, was once a pupil. The Oratory School later became St. Philip's Grammar School and is now a sixth form college. The church there, built early in the present century as a memorial to Newman, is in the Italian Renaissance style. Other churches in the locality are predominantly Victorian.

For those privileged to live within Edgbaston's extensive conservation area, there are the rare advantages of a semi-rural environment combined with all the amenities offered by a big city. There are good shopping

Calthorpe Road, Edgbaston in 1910

Metchley Park Road in May, 1933

A road-sweeper's seat in Church Road, Edgbaston at the junction of Carpenter Road. In the 19th century, sweepers could sometimes earn a shilling a day from their efforts

A surviving cast-iron oil-lamp standard in Calthorpe Road, dating from when the road was opened in 1815

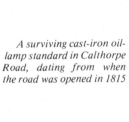

facilities and medical services and a wide choice of schools and churches. There are also hotels, public-houses, parkland, playing fields and the incomparable Botanical Gardens. By contrast, an area of some 90 acres around Five Ways has been given over to the needs of commerce and the professions, with office accommodation ranging from refurbished Georgian houses to air-conditioned tower-blocks.

Numerous additions have been made to the University at Edgbaston since its opening in 1909, including accommodation for a number of science faculties. Due to the acquisition of a considerable amount of extra land the site now has what one commentator described as 'a remarkably extensive and open campus for a university within an industrial city.' The nine-acre site of the Midland Headquarters of the B.B.C., built in the late 'sixties, was once the site of the Pebble Mill. Prior to the start of building there, the damp field was used for grazing horses.

Edgbaston's only cinema is the triple-screen *Bristol* in Bristol Road, which was opened in 1937. The only other local cinema, *The Edgbaston* in

'The Edgbaston' in Monument Road, first opened its doors in 1928

Monument Road, first opened its doors in 1928. It survived for over 40 years before being demolished. Sporting facilities are first-rate. Edgbaston Golf Course is one of the finest in the country, set amidst beautiful surroundings. The county ground at Edgbaston, home of the Warwickshire County Cricket Club, is known everywhere that the game is played. It celebrated its centenary in June, 1986. One of the Club's sponsors in 1886 was the then Mayor of Birmingham, Alderman Thomas Martineau, later Sir Thomas Martineau. In May 1986, coinciding with the centenary year, his great-grandson, Councillor Denis Martineau, was made Lord Mayor of Birmingham, and in the course of the 1986 season, Dennis Amiss became the only Warwickshire cricketer to achieve the rare distinction of scoring one-hundred first-class centuries. Tennis enthusiasts are catered for by the Tally Ho Lawn Tennis Club in Edgbaston Road, situated on the site of Edgbaston's manorial mill, and by the Edgbaston Priory Club in Sir Harry's Road.

The Botanical Gardens in Westbourne Road is a place of enduring interest and enjoyment all the year round. Loudon's masterpiece, (see page 37), with its beautiful, south-facing site, its glasshouses, its exotic plants and birds, its rose, alpine and rhododendron gardens and its children's play area caters for varying tastes. There is the additional attraction of a 2½ acre adjunct to the gardens, in which a nature reserve has been created, where students and school children can study wild nature without the necessity of going to far-away places to do so.

Another spot where nature survives in great diversity is in the wooded conservancy area around Edgbaston Pool, a fact acknowledged by its having been designated as a Site of Special Scientific Interest in 1973. In an age when nature everywhere is under threat perhaps the most eloquent tribute to Edgbaston is to be found here, where, quite remarkably, no less than 130 species of birds have been recorded, most of them identified by boy-naturalists from nearby King Edward VI School.

'The King's Head Hotel', Hagley Road

'The White Swan' in Harborne Road

'The Plough and Harrow Hotel' in 1986, little changed in appearance over the years

Hagley Road near the Ivy Bush before tree-felling and road-widening

EDGBASTON GROUND CENTENARY 1886 — 1986

WARWICKSHIRE COUNTY CRICKET CLUB

FIRST KNOWN PHOTOGRAPH OF PLAY IN PROGRESS, EDGBASTON 1899

A post-card commemorating the centenary of the County Ground at Edgbaston
(Copyright: Ken Kelly)

Hagley Road in 1986

Five Ways Underpass, 1986

The River Rea, viewed from the bridge in Edgbaston Road, 1986

Edgbaston Old Church, in 1986

Moseley Hall

CHAPTER VIII

Near Neighbours

THE PARISHES AROUND Edgbaston have always been eclipsed by their aristocratic neighbour, and in token of the fact Moseley has been described as 'a lesser Edgbaston'. It once lay within the parish of Kings Norton and its church was then merely a chapel-of-ease. This fifteenth century edifice was rebuilt in 1780 and greatly altered in the early nineteenth century. Further work was carried out in 1910 and again in the 1950s, following damage caused during the Second World War.

Unlike Edgbaston, Moseley has the focal point of a village centre, with a cluster of buildings around the church. The coming of the railway in 1867, however, did much to erode Moseley's village image and ensure its transition into a pleasant Birmingham suburb. Moseley Hall, like Edgbaston Hall, was a target for rioters in 1791. It fared less well than Edgbaston Hall and was set on fire, together with its outhouses and hay-stacks. It was rebuilt in 1799 and later became the home of Richard Cadbury, who gave it in 1890 for use as a children's home.

In 1873 Cannon Hill Fields at Moseley were given to Birmingham by Miss Louisa Ann Ryland and converted into Cannon Hill Park. Miss Ryland, a member of an old Birmingham family, was a retiring, self-effacing lady who had been disappointed in love. She declined to have the park named after her, and at her request it was opened without any formal ceremony. An extension to the park was made in 1897, when Lord Calthorpe and Sir John Holder each gave seven acres of land to Birmingham Corporation on the understanding that the course of the River Rea should be straightened in the area. Queen's Ride was then made, the intention being that it should have a similar role to that of Rotten Row in Hyde Park, London.

Harborne was a Staffordshire village until it was annexed by Birmingham in 1891. It now enjoys the status of another pleasant suburb, where numerous pockets of natural beauty remain. The leafy Moor Pool Estate is one such place. The rhymester who wrote the couplet:

Hungry Harborne, proud and poor,
A washer woman at every door.

'Moseley has the focal point of a village centre, with a cluster of buildings around the Church'

probably had in mind the fact that local women once did their own washing in the soft waters of Moor Pool, as well as that of the prosperous inhabitants of Edgbaston.

Only the fifteenth century tower remains of Harborne's parish church, which was largely rebuilt in 1867. One building which looks older than it is is the Bluecoat School in Somerset Road. It was built in 1930 to replace the eighteenth century school which stood beside St. Philip's Churchyard in Birmingham, and its design is redolent of that period.

Harborne's most distinguished inhabitant was David Cox, the water-colour artist. Born in Heath Mill Lane, Deritend in 1783, the son of a blacksmith, he lived from 1841 until his death in 1859 at Greenfield House in Harborne. He is buried in the churchyard of the parish church.

Probably, nowhere in Birmingham was there a more unusual society than one at Harborne, where gardeners enjoyed the distinction of growing fine

'The Golden Lion' in Cannon Hill Park

THE GOLDEN LION.

THIS BUILDING IS BELIEVED TO HAVE BEEN THE CLERGY HOUSE AND SCHOOL OF THE GUILD OF DERITEND IT WAS THE SCENE OF BIRMINGHAM'S EARLIEST STEP TOWARDS PUBLIC EDUCATION, AND IN IT JOHN ROGERS THE FIRST TO PRINT A COMPLETE BIBLE IN THE ENGLISH TONGUE AND ALSO THE FIRST MARTYR UNDER QUEEN MARY WAS TAUGHT

BOUGHT BY PRIVATE SUBSCRIPTION AND PRESENTED TO THE BATHS & PARKS COMMITTEE OF THE CITY COUNCIL IT WAS BY THEM RE-ERECTED HERE IN THE YEAR 1911. AS A MEMORIAL OF THE EARLY PUBLIC LIFE OF OUR CITY.

ALDERMAN W. H. BOWATER, J.P. LORD MAYOR.
COUNCILLOR N. G. READING J.P. CHAIRMAN.
WILLIAM H. MORTER, SUPERINTENDENT.

Rear view of 'Golden Lion'

High Street, Harborne, c. 1905

gooseberries. In furtherance of that skill they formed a Gooseberry Growers' Society at the Green Man in 1815, which survived well into the present century.

The Victorian St. John's Church, Ladywood stands proud in the middle of a redevelopment area. Due to its opened-up surroundings, caused partly by war damage and partly by large-scale demolition in the post-war era, it has considerable visual charm. When the plague reached Birmingham from London in the seventeenth century—said to have been brought from the metropolis in a box of clothes—a large pit was dug near where this church now stands. It occupied an acre of waste land and here were buried the plague victims. The spot was formerly shown on maps as 'the pest ground'.

Nearby, in Waterworks Road is an unusual 96-foot, six-storey building, The Monument, known widely as 'Perrott's Folly'. It was built by a local landowner, John Perrott, in 1758. Described as 'a slender brick-built octagon', The Monument, where Perrott entertained his friends, originally stood in isolation, commanding fine views across open country. The

Moor Pool, Harborne

*The Monument, a 96-foot building
in Waterworks Road, known
widely as 'Perrott's Folly'*

touching story that he built it so that he could view from a distance the grave of a dead lover appears to be of doubtful authenticity.

Rotton Park has a valid claim to antiquity, for in 1307 it is recorded that three men were indicted before Warwick Assize for poaching in 'the Parc de Rotton juxta Birmingham'. The Park once covered a large tract of land bordering on Edgbaston, Ladywood and Winson Green, including the present-day Summerfield Park. Both Rotton Park and Ladywood suffered the consequences of air-raids during the Second World War, resulting in loss of life and damage to property.

Over the years a variety of activities have taken place in and around Rotton Park Reservoir. These include angling, sailing and jogging around the perimeter. A roller-skating rink later became the Tower Ballroom and after the last war Butlin's built a miniature fun-fair on its banks.

Rotton Park's best known figure is that of Joseph Gillott, penmaker-extraordinary and art connoisseur, who bought the Rotton Park estate. He collected pictures, violins and precious stones. In addition to his ownership of Rotton Park he also had a mansion in Westbourne Road, Edgbaston.

Just beyond the Kings Head Hotel is Lightwoods Park, in the grounds of which stands the former home of Sir Francis Galton, F.R.S., African explorer, founder of the science of eugenics and cousin of Charles Darwin. His research led him into many fields of knowledge, including psychology, anthropology, meteorology and criminology, in which science he developed the method of identification by means of finger-prints.

———————

Edgbaston's history and topography is well matched by that of its near neighbours and those people both in and around Edgbaston, who have contributed to the story cover a wide spectrum in the fields of art, literature, science, medicine and politics.

Rotton Park Reservoir

The house in Lightwoods Park, once the home of Sir Francis Galton, F.R.S.

Bibliography

The Antiquities of Warwickshire (1656)   Sir William Dugdale

The History of Birmingham (1781)   William Hutton

A History of Edgbaston (1914)   Philip B. Chatwin

Victoria County History of Warwickshire   Edited by L.F. Salzman
(Vol. 7) (1947)

Portrait of Birmingham (1970)   Vivian Bird

History of Birmingham   Anthony Sutcliffe and
Vol. 3—Birmingham 1939-1970 (1974)   Roger Smith

Lords and Landlords   David Cannadine
The Aristocracy and the Towns,
1774-1967 (1980)

Some Local Worthies

Elihu Burritt, (1810-1879) was, for a time, the American Consul in Birmingham, when he lived in Victoria Road, Harborne. He was reputed to have known fifty languages. He was author of *Walks in the Black Country,* (1868), in which he described Edgbaston Old Church as 'one of the most beautiful little churches in England.'

Geo. Cadbury (1839-1922). A member of the distinguished Quaker family, cocoa and chocolate manufacturers, he was born in Calthorpe Road, Edgbaston. In 1879 he founded the model factory and housing estate at Bournville, for his workers, the plans of which he prepared himself.

Edward Capern, (1819-1894) was known as 'the Postman Poet'. He was a Devonshire man, but lived for a considerable time in Harborne. He is remembered for his lines on 'Love Lane', now Richmond Hill Road, Edgbaston:

> *But no vestige of the bankside lingers now,*
> *or gate to show*
> *The track of the old vanished lane of love's*
> *sweet long ago*

Joseph Chamberlain (1836-1914) was a Radical politician. As Mayor of Birmingham from 1873 to 1876 he did much to improve living counditions in the town. He was elected M.P. for West Birmingham in 1874. He became the first Chancellor of Birmingham University and his name is commemorated in that of the Chamberlain Clock Tower at Bournbrook, (see Chapter VII).

Neville Chamberlain, (1869-1940) was a son of Joseph Chamberlain. He was born at Edgbaston and his home was in Westbourne Road. He was Member of Parliament for Ladywood from 1918 to 1929 and from 1929 he represented Edgbaston. After holding a number of cabinet posts he became Prime Minister in 1937 and it was he who announced that Britain was at war with Germany in 1939.

David Cox, (1783-1859), the famous water-colour artist, was born in Heath Mill Lane, Birmingham, the son of a blacksmith. He lived for much of his life in Harborne. (See Chapter VIII).

Sir Francis Galton F.R.S. (1822-1911) was a many sided genius who is remembered today as the founder of the science of eugenics. He was educated at King Edward VI School, Birmingham and Trinity College, Cambridge. His family home was Lightwoods House in the grounds of Lightwoods Park. The house has survived a serious threat of demolition in the 'sixties. (See Chapter VIII).

Joseph Gillott, (1799-1873) shared with Josiah Mason the credit of having perfected the steel pen and was known as 'the Prince of Penmakers.' He had an estate at Rotton Park and a mansion in Westbourne Road, Edgbaston.

Sir Oliver Lodge, (1851-1940) was a distinguished physicist. He was also a spiritualist who claimed that he had communicated with his dead son, Raymond, who was killed during the Great War. He lived in Westbourne Road, Edgbaston.

John Henry Shorthouse, (1834-1903) was a Quaker. He was author of *John Inglesant,* (1881), described as an historical romance. He lived in Wellington Road, Edgbaston and in the grounds of his house there was a folly, known as 'Edgbaston Castle'.

John Henry Newman, (1801-1890) was a convert to Catholicism who became a Cardinal. He composed 'Lead Kindly Light' and founded the Oratory at Edgbaston.

Joseph Sturge, (1793-1859) was a pacifist and a campaigner against slavery. His statue is at Five Ways.

John Ronald Reuel Tolkien, (1892-1973) was an academic who turned to fantasy and wrote tales for his children, from which evolved his famous book, *The Lord of the Rings.* He lived at various times in Hall Green and Kings Heath and on a wall of the City Estates Department in Hagley Road, Edgbaston there is a blue plaque commemorating the fact that he lived in a house near there from 1902 to 1910.

Henry Van Wart, (1783-1873) was an American by birth, a Dutchman by descent and an Englishman by adoption. He was a successful businessman and a Birmingham alderman who lived in the town for almost seventy years. For a part of that time his home was in Calthorpe Road, Edgbaston. There he was visited frequently by his brother-in-law, Washington Irving, whose masterpiece, *Rip Van Winkle,* was written while staying at an earlier home of Van Wart in the Birmingham Jewellery District.

William Withering, (1741-1799) was the doctor who discovered the medical uses of the foxglove. He was tenant of Edgbaston Hall during the Birmingham Riots of 1791. (See Chapter IV).

Henry Van Wart, an American by birth, who, while living in Calthorpe Road, was visited frequently by his brother-in-law, Washington Irving

Washington Irving's masterpiece, 'Rip Van Winkle', was written while he was staying at an earlier home of Van Wart in the Birmingham Jewellery district

LOCAL BOOKS
by local authors

THE ROYAL TOWN of SUTTON COLDFIELD
A Commemorative History
by Douglas V. Jones

Running to 208 pages and covering the period from Saxon times up till 1974, when the Royal Town of Sutton Coldfield was amalgamated with Birmingham this is a warm human story of local people, events and landmarks.

SUTTON COLDFIELD 1974-1984 The Story of a Decade
by Douglas V. Jones

A lavishly illustrated Chronicle which recalls the many changes to the face of Sutton since its merger with Birmingham, with a Pictorial Supplement, *Sutton in 1984.*

SUTTON PARK Its History and Wildlife
by Douglas V. Jones

Profusely illustrated with a wide selection of old and new pictures most of which have not previously been published, complete with centrefold map, and detailed with three interesting walks short enough for the casual walker to take at leisure.

STEAMING UP TO SUTTON How the Birmingham to Sutton Coldfield Railway Line was built in 1862
written by Roger Lea

Every day thousands travel on the railway line between Sutton and Birmingham, without giving much thought to its origins and history. This is the fascinating story.

MEMORIES OF A TWENTIES CHILD
by Douglas V. Jones

A nostalgic trip into one man's childhood and youth during the years between the wars. The book is a profusely illustrated reminder of the age of steam, gas-lamps, crystal-sets and tramcars.

DURATION MAN 1939-46 My War
by Douglas V. Jones

An enthralling sequel to "Memories of a Twenties Child"
This is the story of some of those who fought the good fight against red tape, boredom and gloom in places where all three were often present. If from time to time it may appear that soldiering is a mug's game, then the reader must draw his own conclusions. 144 pages, fully illustrated.

ROUND ABOUT THE ROTUNDA Four Decades of Life in and around Birmingham 1945-1987
by Douglas V. Jones

This sequel to *Memories of a Twenties Child* and *Duration Man* presents an enthralling and evocative picture of Birmingham in transition during the last four decades reminding us on the way of the many interesting landmarks which have now disappeared. Illustrated with over a hundred photographs of the passing scene.